Introduction

D1714594

Three weeks after Lyndon B. Johnson was overwhelmingly elected the "peace" president of the United States, he carried out one of the most brutal and cynical aggressions against an oppressed people in the history of world colonialism—the November 1964 paratroop "rescue" attack on Stanleyville.

The purpose of these articles is to examine, however briefly, the historical background of this attack, its immediate causes, and its effect on Africa. Even so brief an examination reveals the interests of the Western powers in the Congo, and the variety of tactics, including United Nations intervention, through which the colonial powers act to maintain their interests.

However, the most important lesson of this study, by far, is the lesson of the total hypocrisy of the Democratic Party's claim to "peaceful" resolution of international problems. The massacres inflicted against the black Congolese by the Johnson administration vividly—and tragically—refute these claims.

And, as was shown by the bombings of North Vietnam which followed the Congolese crisis in a matter of weeks, such aggressions are not the exception. They are becoming the rule.

Dick Roberts
New York
February 27, 1965

Background to the Congo

The Congo has been the scene of unceasing turbulence since June 30th, 1960, the day the Congolese gained formal independence from Belgium. Real independence, however, consisting of self-determination in all spheres of life, could not be obtained simply through a change in the political relationships between the Congo and Belgium. This change only set the stage for a new and deeper struggle, the struggle for *economic* independence.

Not only Belgium, but France, England, and particularly the United States had no intention of allowing their vast economic holdings in the Congo to be jeopardized by the new Republic. Increasingly, as the Congolese struggle became one for economic independence, these foreign powers and their agents within the Congo became formidable opponents of independence. The deepening struggle drove divisions into the Congolese peoples, widely separating those who fought for complete independence from those who desired to remain within the economic confines of world capitalist investment.

The partisans of independence were further divided on

tactical questions: Could independence be obtained peacefully, through parliamentary means? Or was it necessary to engage in armed struggle against the imperialist powers and their Congolese puppets?

A few years is a very short time for a revolutionary movement to learn the answers to these questions. Their opponents, the imperialist nations, have developed the political instruments of economic exploitation over decades. In the Congo, they employed a variety of tactics in their overall strategy of holding Congolese mineral wealth to the world capitalist market.

Foreign investment in the Congo

The major foreign economic holdings in the Congo are in the vast mineral enterprises of the province of Katanga, which in 1960 realized about 60% of the total Congo revenues. Most of Katanga's mineral reserves are owned and mined by a giant U.S.-British-Belgian controlled corporation, the *Union Miniere du Haut Katanga,* (UMHK). In 1960, with annual sales of $200 million, UMHK produced 60% of the uranium in the West, 73% of the cobalt, and 10% of the copper, and had in the Congo 24 affiliates including hydroelectric plants, chemical factories and railways.

The Cold War and nuclear arms race had been very profitable for Congolese enterprises. Besides mineral industries, many other factories had been built by foreign capitalists. Belgium invested over $3 billion in the Congo, and the U.S. about $½ billion—much of it coming from the Rockefeller family who purchased everything from pineapple plantations to car companies.

At first sight, it would appear that the U.S. and Belgium had common interest in preserving the Congolese market, and in the last analysis this is true. But in the initial period of independence, U.S. investors attempted to take

3

advantage of the fact that Belgium would lose her political reins on the Congo. Just prior to 1960, U.S. capitalists greatly increased their Congo holdings, and they continued to do so through last year. David Rockefeller, for example, bought the bauxite industry, Bauxicongo, in 1959; and the Rockefellers have increased their share of UMHK as well as other large enterprises.

Other American corporations have put their fingers in the Congo grab-bag, including American Metal Climax (Arthur Dean, U.S. delegate to the Geneva conference on disarmament was a vice-president) and the Tempelsman and Son (Adlai Stevenson was president). From 1961 to 1963, U.S. investments doubled to $1.2 billion—nearly the amount presently invested by the U.S. in Brazil.

But the United States interests in the Congo are not uniform. In the crucial copper industry, there has been a world overproduction of copper, amounting to about 10% of the world produce, the same amount as is produced in Katanga. Thus giant copper industries in this country, like Kennecott and Anaconda, which get most of their copper from Chile, would just as soon see the Katanga copper industry destroyed, as fall into the hands of a competitor like Rockefeller.

Swedish capitalists also have large holdings in competitive copper enterprises. Bo Hammarskjold, elder brother of the late UN Secretary General, was on the board of directors of the Swedish controlled Liberian Iron Ore, Ltd., a corporation which found American allies in the desire to diminish Katangese competition.

With such an investment pattern, it is easy to see why the imperialist nations were interested in ensuring their control of Congolese mineral wealth; but it is also easy to see why the tactics of maintaining this control might differ between nations, and within the nations, themselves.

Congo independence and UN intervention

Upon achieving political independence, the Congolese held a general election to determine the membership of their democratic parliament. The majority of seats were won by the largest independence force, the Congolese National Movement, headed by the revered leader of the independence struggle, Patrice Lumumba. Lumumba was named Prime Minister.

However, no sooner had Lumumba been elected, than Belgium began to take steps to weaken his government. The Belgians had forced the Congolese to allow them to maintain an army and air bases in the Congo, ostensibly for "mutual cooperation." A week after independence, when Congolese soldiers demonstrated against their Belgian officers with a demand for pay and rank raises, Belgian troops fired on the demonstrators. Lumumba, in turn, removed the Belgian officers, and appointed Josef Kasavubu commander-in-chief.

The Belgians quickly exploited the situation they had provoked. Claiming that Lumumba was inspiring "racial hatred" and couldn't be trusted to govern the Congo, they rushed in new troops, and separated Katanga from the Congo Republic—using Moise Tshombe, a wealthy plantation owner and businessman as their Katanga front man.

In this crisis, Lumumba correctly accused the Belgians of having "carefully prepared the secession of Katanga," and asked for the immediate help of the United Nations . . . a fatal error, as Lumumba himself learned, all too soon. The United States completely dominated the UN.

Seizing the opportunity to extend foreign military control in the Congo, the U.S. pushed the UN to meet Lumumba's request, and the UN sped troops to the Congo July 14. They had no intentions of driving Belgium out of the Congo. Temporary commander of UN forces, Alexander, flatly stated, "friendly relations would . . . be established" with the Belgians.

It was almost immediately apparent to Lumumba that the UN was double-dealing, and he requested outside support from the Soviet Union, to intervene "should the Western camp not stop its aggression."

By July 30 the Belgians had built up a force of over 10,000 troops, and the UN army had refused to enter Katanga. On August 2nd, Antoine Gizenga, Lumumba's right-hand man and delegate to the UN, told Hammarskjold:

> We do not understand that we, victims of aggression, who are at home here, are being systematically disarmed [by the UN force] while the aggressors, the Belgians, who are the conquerors here, are permitted to keep their weapons and their means of inflicting death.

In Katanga, Belgian troops crushed uprisings of Congolese soldiers and miners, and protected Tshombe's efforts to suppress opposition from minority leaders in the Katanga parliament. The UN closed broadcasting stations in Leopoldville and commanded Lumumba not to meddle in Katanga.

According to Under-Secretary Ralph Bunche, the UN's mission was to "pacify and then to administer the Congo. . . ." From the very outset, it was clear that the UN did not recognize the duly elected government of Lumumba, and intended to restore a pro-Belgian, pro-U.S. government.

Influence of world pressure

However, world pressure, not only from the Soviet bloc, but from newly independent African nations which threatened to draw their armies out of the UN force, demanded that the UN live up to Lumumba's request. At this point, the tactics of U.S. and Belgian imperialism temporarily diverged.

The United States recognized the necessity of a temporary maneuver to avoid international criticism. World opinion had a particularly significant effect because the September 1960 opening of the UN was scheduled to be addressed by Nasser, Tito and Nehru, the leaders of the neutral nations; by Khrushchev; by Toure of Guinea and Nkrumah of Ghana; and by Fidel Castro.

This array of world leaders could have had an unusually damaging effect on the U.S. public image—protector of the free world; and this image could only be protected to a limited extent by restricting Khrushchev and Castro to a confined area of New York, and preventing them from appearing on TV.

Consequently, the United States pressured the UN to end Belgian occupation. On August 21, Hammarskjold told the Security Council: "The Belgian chapter in the history of the Congo in its earlier forms is ended. The UN . . . is in charge of order and security."

Lumumba's murder

By this time the Congo crisis had had a second important divisive effect, this time on the Congolese themselves. Elements of the next largest political party after the Congolese National Movement, the Abako Party, led by Kasavubu, threw their cards in with United States interests.

Kasavubu, who had been powerless in the original government, now took sides against Lumumba, demanding that he be ousted, and sending a separate delegation to the UN. This gave the UN a considerably stronger hand in the Congo, even though many UN members, led by Nkrumah, held that Lumumba was the head of the only legitimate

7

Congo government.

Castro, who delivered his famous UN speech indicting the U.S. for support of Batista throughout the Cuban revolution, charged that Col. Mobutu, Kasavubu's military aide, had been advised and encouraged by U.S. officials.

Unfortunately, Lumumba continued to rely on appeals to the UN, undoubtedly supported in this futile effort by the Soviet Union. Khrushchev held the ill-advised position that "Dag, not the UN," was responsible. Instead of exposing the UN as a pawn in the hands of the State Department, and building an independent military force in the Congo to protect the legitimate government, Lumumba and his Soviet allies played into the hands of the imperialists and Kasavubu.

On September 5, Lumumba was summarily removed from office, Soviet representatives were ordered out of the country, and a military dictatorship was established under Col. Mobutu. In the UN, the independent nations strongly opposed these moves, blaming them on Belgium, and demanding the restoration of Lumumba—all to little avail. Overridden by the U.S. and her UN lackeys, their motion to restore Lumumba was defeated November 22 by a vote of 53-to-24.

Again Lumumba temporized, this time fatally. Remaining in Leopoldville until the end of November, his belated effort to escape was doomed to fail. On December 1st, Lumumba was seized, publicly mauled in a truck before U.S. TV cameras and imprisoned in Leopoldville; this while UN forces stood by.

On January 18, Kasavubu, in return for a "round-table conference" with Tshombe, handed prisoner Lumumba over to the Belgian stooge. A January 18 AP dispatch reported that on Lumumba's arrival at the Katanga airport, Swedish-UN soldiers watched while "Lumumba and the other two

Patrice Lumumba (right) with aides, just before they were murdered.

were dragged off the plane. . . . They were clubbed, hit in the face with rifle butts, kicked and pummeled."

And, as it became clear upon UN investigation months later, Lumumba and his two aides were subsequently murdered. Their deaths were reported by Tshombe, February 12.

Tshombe and Katanga

During these few months, the lessons of United Nations intervention were slowly being assimilated by Congolese revolutionaries. Gizenga established the legitimate government's headquarters in Stanleyville, and more and more Congolese joined in open rebellion. It was obvious that the provisional government of Kasavubu would not last without reconciliation with Katanga, and the U.S. pressed for a federated Congo government which would include Katanga.

The U.S. publicly broke with Belgium and forced the UN to demand an end of Katanga secession, which the Security Council adopted February 21st, 1961—eight months after their intervention to "defend" the Congo Republic.

But Belgium, and those U.S. interests which composed the Katanga lobby, refused to go along with this maneuver. Here, a movement cropped up calling itself the "Committee to Aid the Katanga Freedom Fighters," and Tshombe, who had been bolstered by Belgian troops until their forced removal, set about to build an army which could resist the UN, financed by Belgium. With no support from the Congolese, however, Tshombe recruited his "freedom fighters" from rightist white rabble throughout the world. A February 5, 1961, AP dispatch described them:

> These 'mercenaries' are being joined every day by new soldier-adventurers. Lured by high pay, they have come from the United States [Cuban exiles], Britain, France [ex-Foreign Legionnaires], West Germany [ex-SS men], . . . South Africa [fascists], Rhodesia—and, of course, Belgium. Some of the better types become officers, but the others are undisciplined, untidy, rowdy and ruthless. . . .
>
> One Frenchman confided in a melancholy moment: 'People don't like us. We get good pay for killing women and children.'

The battle in Katanga, which lasted until January 1963, had other sordid aspects which were exposed by the Belgian and English press. The UN, for example, used 1,000 pound blockbusters on Katangese industrial centers, civilians, and hospitals—military weapons well suited to destroying large industry (competitors), members of the House of Commons pointed out, but hardly applicable to the battle against Tshombe's small mercenary forces. Such goings-on had little press coverage in this country.

Revolutionary defeats: 1962

What is obvious in retrospect, that the apparent break of Tshombe from the Kasavubu government, and subsequent "round-table conferences" between them, were maneuvers by the imperialist powers to crush the revolutionaries, was not apparent to many of the Lumumbists.

In February of 1961, Kasavubu ended the Mobutu dictatorship and appointed Joseph Ileo and Cyrille Adoula heads of a new government, patterned after the U.S. federation plan. Tshombe and Kasavubu met in March, 1961, at Tananarive, Malagasy Republic, and invited Gizenga to attend to join a federation.

Although Gizenga, already in control of large portions of the Congo, refused to go to the Tananarive conference, he later attempted to make peace with Kasavubu. In mid-1962, while the UN was fighting Tshombe, Gizenga achieved a detente with Kasavubu.

Again the Lumumbists had incorrectly appraised the real intentions of the imperialist controlled Kasavubu regime, and they suffered a new setback. Kasavubu turned round and arrested Gizenga, threw him in prison, and disarmed the Stanleyville forces. Gizenga remained in prison until June, 1964.

End of UN occupation

By January, 1963, after nearly two years of battle in Katanga, the United Nations forces had gained virtual control of the province. Attempts to reinstate Tshombe in the Kasavubu-Adoula government, which would have satisfied both Belgium and the United States, proved unsuccessful, and Tshombe was "forced" into exile. His mercenary army was temporarily shelved in the neighboring Portuguese colony of Angola.

With Gizenga in jail, the Adoula government attempted to build a stable base for neocolonialist investment. Three years of struggle had decimated the Congolese economy— inflation was rampant in Leopoldville, and thousands of refugees from the countryside poured into the city looking for work.

At the same time, however, the Congolese people remained staunch Lumumbists, and guerrilla struggles emerged in several different areas. In the Leopoldville shantytown, where thousands of jobless refugees were huddled together, virtually every hut bore portraits of Lumumba, and it was impossible for Adoula's police to enter the area in uniform.

It was clear that Adoula's attempts to attract foreign capital (see his January 28, 1964, advertisement in the *New York Times*, "Private Enterprise in the Congo") were not alone sufficient to hold up the faltering government. But it was also impossible, given the world pressure on the UN, to turn the "anti-Katangese" UN army into a direct "anti-Lumumbist" force. Standing by while Lumumba was murdered and Gizenga was imprisoned was one thing; openly fighting the Lumumbists on three fronts, quite another.

For these reasons, the United States was forced, once again, to alter its Congo policy: the United Nations army would be replaced by . . . Tshombe's mercenaries.

Tshombe's return

In his brief "exile" from the Congo, Tshombe was well groomed for a new role in Congo politics. Over the summer of 1963, Tshombe conferred in Brussels with Foreign Minister Paul-Henri Spaak and the U.S. Ambassador. Harriman was sent to address Spaak and the Belgian trust *La*

Societe Generale, the largest shareholder in UMHK; and the U.S. and Belgium agreed to merge forces. A new maneuver was at hand.

On June 30, 1964, United Nations forces were pulled out of the Congo, and Tshombe returned—as the "saviour" of Congolese independence. He replaced Adoula, and proclaimed that the "National Congolese Army" would be able to handle the "rebels." As evidence of his sincerity, Tshombe released Gizenga.

Two days later he brought his mercenary hooligans out of hiding and called upon the U.S. for military assistance.

The Congo revolution today

A literally complete press blackout of Congolese guerrilla efforts, between the fall of Gizenga in mid-1962, and early 1964, makes it impossible to trace in detail the revolutionary struggle during the latter period of UN occupation.

It was evident by last February that there was extensive fighting in Kwilu, headed by Pierre Mulele, who had been minister of education in the Lumumba government. By early June, the liberation struggle had opened up two other fronts: Gaston Soumialot fought in the eastern province of Kivu, and occupied Uvira May 19; and a third force fought in Northern Katanga, gained control of the whole shore of Lake Tanganyika and captured Albertville and Baudouinville in late June.

Obviously, Mobutu's army was in continual retreat. There have been many reports that his Congolese soldiers refuse to fight their brothers, and give up without effort. By early July, Stanleyville had been recaptured by the Lumumbists, and a new government established, headed by Christophe Gbenye. Exactly how much control Gbenye's government has over all the guerrilla fighters is unclear.

Although the United States did not admit military support of the mercenaries until October, first reports of U.S. military assistance appeared in June. According to the *New York Times*, 2 T-28's, flown by Cuban exiles, were being used by Mobutu's army, June 13. Mobutu was reported to be battling guerrilla forces numbering 5,000 to 7,000, average age, about 20!

Since that time, the U.S. has supplied Tshombe with a paratroop contingent, army counterinsurgency "experts" and 33 known additional aircraft, including B-26 bombers. Against even such minimal modern weapons, the guerrillas, without any anti-aircraft guns whatsoever, and using the most crude weapons—spears and bows and arrows—have been reported to be retreating.

Conclusion

To a certain extent, we can see that the story of the Vietnamese war is being repeated in the Congo: after a series of maneuvers to maintain "friendly" quasi-democratic governments in the Congo, the U.S. has ended up in a position of open support for another hated dictator—and in this case, one who cannot get his own people to fight the oppressive war. As in Vietnam, U.S. support includes guns, dollars, and . . . "advisers."

To date, it is by no means apparent that the Lumumbists have organizational and programmatic unity, capable of opposing the overwhelming odds of the U.S. military intervention. There is no guarantee that there will not be new compromises between certain Lumumbist leaders and the puppet regime. The great loss of Patrice Lumumba has not been salvaged by the appearance of a new nationally recognized leader.

But it is also clear that throughout the course of the struggle, there have been groups of revolutionaries who refuse to submit to the rule of imperialist controlled governments. These fighters maintained unrelenting struggle against the Kasavubu regime, and they continue to oppose the Tshombe regime. It is from their cadres that a viable and organized revolutionary movement can emerge, capable of ending once and for all imperialist subjugation of the Congo.

The U.S. vs. Africa

On November 24, 1964, the combined forces of United States, Belgian and British imperialism desperately attempted to stem the tide of the African revolution by an unprecedentedly brutal attack on the stronghold of the Congolese liberation struggle in Stanleyville. This attack, which was systematically supported by an equally unprecedented barrage of racist propaganda in the world imperialist press, not only failed to achieve its desired end—it thrust the African revolution onto a higher level of unity and resistance.

From early in 1961, with the murder of Patrice Lumumba, until late November, 1964—a period of almost four years—the Congolese liberation struggle developed slowly, suffering many setbacks. In the space of only six weeks, this revolution became one of the major battlefronts against world imperialism.

In November last year, the Congo freedom forces, armed only with spears and bows and arrows, attempted to oppose a mercenary army equipped with the most advanced weapons of guerrilla warfare. By the third week of January, this year, the same movement had become well organized, well armed, and showed itself able to oppose the mercenaries and even to turn them back.

Six weeks before, they fought alone. Now they were materially supported by three African nations as well as the Soviet Union. In the United Nations, independent African nations joined forces to launch an uncompromising attack on U.S. foreign policy; in Africa, they made major steps toward providing support to the Congolese liberation front.

The Congo: summer 1964

On June 30, 1964, the four-year period of UN occupation of the Congo ended, and Moise Tshombe, who had been in exile for a year, returned to the Congo as Premier. During this year's absence, Tshombe had been carefully prepared by the United States and Belgium to fulfill a role which the previous heads of the puppet-Leopoldville government had proved unable to fulfill. It was Tshombe's job to crush once and for all the Lumumbist opposition in the Congo.

Since early 1964, the Lumumbists had been in open struggle on several Congolese fronts. Pierre Mulele, who had been minister of education in the Lumumba government, headed a struggle in Kwilu; Gaston Soumialot fought in Kiva and had taken several large cities; and a third force in Northern Katanga gained control of the whole shore of Lake Tanganyika and had in late June captured Albertville and Baudouinville.

In this period, the Leopoldville army, headed by Colonel Mobutu, was in continual retreat before the Congolese freedom fighters. Mobutu's men refused to fire at their black brothers, and many deserted to the side of freedom. By July, the liberation movement had recaptured Stanleyville—where four years earlier Lumumba's right-hand man, Antoine Gizenga, had established the headquarters of the Congolese government.

White mercenaries in the service of puppet Tshombe. On the left is Vic Oglethorpe of South Africa; on the right, Dougie Lord of England. Tshombe cannot find enough black Africans to fight for him, so he has hired a band of scum that includes Cuban counter-revolutionaries, former Nazis, French troops formerly in Algeria, and racists from South Africa.

It was obvious that without foreign pressure the Lumumbists would soon retake the Congo, and end once and for all the imperialists' puppet government in Leopoldville. In order to crush the Lumumbists, Belgium and the United States decided to reinforce the Leopoldville army with the contingent of racist white mercenaries which Tshombe had used to defend the secession of Katanga.

These hired killers had been recruited from terrorist organizations throughout the West and Africa: they were ex-Nazi SS-men; ex-foreign legionnaires who had been in the terrorist OAS which attempted to destroy the Algerian revolution; Cuban counterrevolutionaries recruited in Miami; and South African whites from the police state of Verwoerd. While Tshombe had been touring the capitals of imperialism during his exile, the mercenaries had been stationed in neighboring Angola, with the sanction of the Portuguese dictator Salazar.

Two days after Tshombe returned to the Congo, the mercenaries were sent into the struggle—newly financed and armed with U.S. money and guns. During the course of the next months, they were supplied with U.S. planes, including four C-130 transport planes (*New York Times,* August 13); with 106 Air Force men including 42 paratroopers (*New York Times,* August 15); B-26 bombers (*New York Times,* August 18); T-28's (the so-called trainer plane used in Vietnam as well); rockets, machine guns, and other heavy equipment (*New York Times,* August 25). On August 25, the *New York Times* headlined "Mercenary Unit is Ready to Fight Rebels in Congo," and the Congolese struggle took a decisive turn.

The drive on Stanleyville

The newly equipped Leopoldville army adopted tactics which were new for the present Congolese civil war—but which have been tried and tested in wars of colonial suppression for centuries—namely, rank terrorism. Beginning in late August, and for the subsequent four weeks, the mercenary column drove north on Stanleyville, bombing and pillaging every village in their path, murdering every man, woman and child in sight.

The idea was simple: to so terrorize the Congolese people that they would not dare support the liberation struggle. With their machine guns and bombers they were opposed, if at all, by spears and bows and arrows.

Little of the horrible reality of this drive was permitted to filter through the distorted reportage of the U.S. press; and what little leaked through, was so submerged in racist demagogy as to be barely discernible.

Perhaps a glimmer of the truth was provided by an article in the Sunday *New York Times* magazine section, November 15, by Lloyd Garrison, cutely entitled "White Mercenaries on a Rabbit Hunt." In this lurid article, Garrison explains why the drive on Stanleyville was called a "rabbit hunt" by the mercenaries.

He explains that in the entire course of the drive the mercenaries were unopposed, and that the butchery of civilians was so great, as to turn even the stomachs of the hired killers. "Rabbit hunt" does not describe a military battle against an armed and organized resistance.

In the international press, however, the facts were not completely suppressed. A few, from many descriptions, may be cited: In *Le Nouvel Observateur* (November 26), a French weekly, Emile Lejeune who had been covering the campaign wrote:

> I have seen planes strafe and burn dozens of villages. I have seen tens of thousands of peasants exterminated in the bush by the army of Tshombe. Their corpses are still there; the stench hangs over the streets and fields of a ruined country. . . .
>
> Only mercenaries, come from Rhodesia and South Africa for the pleasure of 'cracking Negro heads,' have made it possible to stop and then to push back the revolutionary wave. . . . The planes

Mercenary belonging to imperialist-organized forces, standing over the body of a slain Congolese fighter.

which supply the regular forces are American, piloted by Americans. The pursuit planes which machine-gun and bombard the *Soumialist* troops and villages which have joined the rebellion are American and piloted by anti-Castro Cubans.

The 'rescue mission'

The paratroop attack on Stanleyville which culminated this drive served Western imperialism in several ways, the least of which—if it was a consideration at all—was the "rescue" of foreign nationals in the Congo. The fact is, and none other than the Belgian Foreign Minister Paul-Henri

Spaak, himself, admitted it, no so-called hostages were killed before the November 24 attack.

Spaak stated, in the UN Security Council: "I have been told, and the argument carries a certain weight, that no one had been killed in Stanleyville before 24 November. This is true—or rather there was a single person killed."

The "rescue mission" served these purposes: First, it was considered essential to reinforce the mercenary campaign to assure the seizure and destruction of Stanleyville. Second, it was a deliberate attempt to intimidate the Organization of African Unity, and thereby sidetrack any possible support of OAU members to the Congolese Liberation Movement. The racist propaganda of the necessity of "saving the white man from the cannibal" served as a cover for the actual operation. In fact, hysteria about "massacres" of the whites was trumped-up well in advance of the actual paratroop drop and served to distract attention from the mercenary drive preceding the attack.

That the mercenaries, alone, would not have been able to take and hold Stanleyville was apparent from the beginning of the mercenary terrorist campaign. By its very nature, this campaign was aimed only at sweeping through the Congolese towns; there was no attempt, nor could there be with limited numbers, to occupy the town once terrorized. Soon after the mercenaries went through towns, people who had fled in their paths, returned. With the support of the paratroopers, the mercenaries hoped to crush all Congolese opposition in and around Stanleyville, and thereby make it possible for a small number of them to remain in the city, and control it. This aspect of the air attack was successful.

The African opposition

The Organization of African Unity responded to the mercenary campaign and anticipated the threat it represented to the Congolese people well in advance of the drive on Stanleyville and the paratroop invasion. Meeting in Addis Ababa in September, the OAU Council of Ministers passed a resolution calling for the establishment of an *ad hoc* commission to deal with the Congo crisis, and demanding all foreign powers to end intervention in the Congo.

Further, the OAU delegated a five-man commission of leading African diplomats to go to Washington and urge President Johnson to withdraw U.S. support of the mercenary army.

From the beginning, this attempt by the OAU to resolve the Congolese crisis on African terms was played down in the press and snubbed in Washington. The White House immediately issued a statement that Johnson would not meet the OAU delegates, and when Joseph Murumbi, Kenya's Minister of State, arrived in the capital he was coolly received by a State Department petty functionary.

Nevertheless, prior to the paratroop attack, the OAU promised to take responsibility for the whites in the Congo, and called an emergency meeting of the *ad hoc* commission in Nairobi to mediate talks between the U.S. Ambassador, Atwood, and Thomas Kanza, representing the Stanleyville government. This meeting took place two days before the "rescue mission."

Once again, however, the imperialists gave lip service to the OAU and went ahead with their predetermined plans. Kanza's promise that the whites would be safe was totally ignored, and the paratroop attack was launched as though the Nairobi meeting had never taken place.

Washington's treatment of the Nairobi commission did not go unnoticed in Africa. Far from producing the desired effect—of splitting the OAU from the Congolese Liberation Movement—it had the opposite effect. Several weeks later

Mrs. Pauline Lumumba, widow of martyred Congolese Premier Patrice Lumumba, shakes hands with Gaston Soumialot, of the Stanleyville government.

one leading African after another took the floor in the UN to denounce Washington's racist and irresponsible attitude to the OAU, and to condemn the U.S. for flagrant intervention in African affairs.

The attack

If there is a difference between the mercenary tactics during the drive on Stanleyville, and the attack on that city reinforced by some 600 Belgian paratroopers, it is only quantitative. In Stanleyville, the combined imperialist forces slaughtered so many thousands of people that no accurate estimate is possible. They left so many bodies on the streets that a typhoid epidemic broke out—in spite of the thousands of bodies burned in mass funeral pyres and other thousands dumped into the river. Such carnage almost staggers the imagination.

Again, the American press has very nearly obliterated these facts from publication. While the description of the typhoid epidemic (UPI) was carried in the New York *Daily News* (December 2), to our knowledge, only one eyewitness account of the actual attack has been printed, and that in the December 5 Baltimore *Afro-American*. The writer is Ed Van Kan, a UPI cameraman: "In the moment it would take me to snap my fingers I saw a squad of Belgian paratroopers kill three Africans who came under their guns.

"And in another incident, the Belgians, rifles ready, stopped an African riding a bicycle through a dusty side street, a bunch of bananas on his head.

"'Are you a Mulelist?' the soldiers demanded.

"'No,' the African replied.

"'You're lying,' one of the Belgians said and shot the man dead. This was Stanleyville, 26 hours after Belgian paratroopers struck with crushing power at the heart of the Congo's rebel empire.

"The Belgian troops are killing or arresting all suspected rebels or rebel supporters. I've seen a lot of bodies, an awful lot of bodies. There is no time to count them. Or desire, in this atmosphere."

Such accounts, however, have not been unavailable to the U.S. press. In the UN Security Council debate, a number of African delegates read mercenaries' and Belgian soldiers' first-hand accounts into the records, such as the following:

> We arrived at the village [on the outskirts of Stanleyville] before nightfall. The women were carrying water and the children were playing and laughing in the streets. We stopped for a while and watched. Then came the order to open fire. Our

new Belgian machine-guns began to fire. Women screamed and fell. Small children were shot down. We just continued to fire. Some of our people threw petrol against the huts and set fire to them. Others threw phosphorous grenades, which transformed the victims into human torches. . . . (Security Council Provisional Verbatim Record, December 30).

The effect

The paratroop attack succeeded only in one sense, that it destroyed the Lumumbist resistance in Stanleyville. Within a week of the attack, the mercenaries stationed in that city were able to crush all opposition. They rounded up hundreds, if not thousands, of those suspected of being in any way connected with the Liberation Movement, and held mass kangaroo court trials, followed by mass executions. (*New York Times,* January 10).

But the major effect of the attack was quite the opposite of what the imperialists intended. The shock of the attack was indeed so great, that far from disorienting and setting back the African revolution as was intended, it thrust Africa into a unified resistance to imperialism, with a deeper commitment to the elimination of foreign interests—and a deeper understanding of the nature of the enemy.

In this country, militant black nationalists, led by Malcolm X, attacked the "rescue mission" as a fraud and pointed out that the real massacres in the Congo—the only ones—were those of the black man by the white armies. Malcolm X pledged solidarity of the Afro-Americans with the Congolese struggle and conducted a series of lectures in Harlem to tell the truth about Africa and to expose the racist lies of the American press.

Eighteen African nations spurred an attack on the

United States in the UN Security Council which left Ambassador Adlai Stevenson blubbering in his chair. It is not possible to begin to summarize the carefully documented and vivid accounts which the African delegates submitted to the UN debate—and they have been virtually ignored by American papers. Suffice it to point out that the precise intentions of the U.S.-Belgian attack were clearly revealed, that the racism of the propaganda about the Congo was completely exposed, and the myth of the rescue operation totally destroyed.

Louis Lansana Beavogui, the delegate from Guinea, called attention to the racist hypocrisy of the U.S. position, December 10:

> In their blind war being carried out under the direction of Belgian, South African and Rhodesian mercenaries, under the protection of United States military planes piloted by Cuban mercenaries recruited and financed by the United States— soldiers of fortune trying to redeem their fiasco in the Bay of Pigs—they have massacred hundreds upon hundreds of defenseless Congolese civilians whom they have called rebels for the needs of their cause. . . .
>
> At the time no indignation was expressed by the so-called civilized Governments and countries which today denounce what they call rebel atrocities. At that time humanitarian reasons were foreign to them. Was it because the thousands of Congolese citizens murdered by the South Africans, the Rhodesians, the Belgians and the Cuban refugee adventurers had dark skins just like the coloured United States citizens murdered in Mississippi?

27

The same afternoon, Tewfik Bouattoura, the Algerian representative, eloquently stated the African position:

> Neither the arms furnished by the United States nor the technicians furnished by Belgium nor the mercenaries had succeeded in reconquering the country. Seized with impatience, Washington and Brussels could think of no other method than to intervene directly with their army, considering that in that way they would give a military trump card to the armed forces directed by the racist mercenaries recruited in South Africa. The pretext was easy to find. It was necessary to protect the lives of the whites. The history of colonization is full of such examples. . . .
>
> The aggression recently perpetrated in the Congo has aroused deep emotion and anxiety in the entire African continent. That aggression tends to reinstate in the world a morality which we had thought was being changed. Some liked to say that gunboat policies, aimed at intimidating smaller countries, were no longer part of our era.
>
> Alas, we are forced to note that things are getting even worse. We are witnessing a return to the direct methods of the eighteenth and nineteenth centuries, illustrated by the intervention of armed troops to protect, acquire or reconquer territories and wealth to which people believed they had a unilateral right. In 1956 it was Suez, today it is the Congo. . . .

But far more important than this parliamentary scuttle, certain African countries led by Algeria came out for direct material support of the Congolese freedom struggle, and within two weeks of the air attack, were shipping arms to the Lumumbists. By December 19 the freedom fighters had rallied their resistance to the mercenary columns, and were reported to have besieged mercenaries in two cities in the northeastern area, Paulis and Bunia. The imperialist attack did not smash the revolution, which is acquiring new strength and support for the struggles ahead.

NEW FROM PATHFINDER

Malcolm X, Black Liberation, and the Road to Workers Power

JACK BARNES

The foundations for the explosive rise of the Black liberation struggle in the U.S. beginning in the mid-1950s were laid by the massive migration of Blacks from the rural South to cities and factories across the continent, drawn by capital's insatiable need for labor power—and cannon fodder for its wars.

Malcolm X emerged from this rising struggle as its outstanding single leader. He insisted that colossal movement was part of a worldwide revolutionary battle for human rights. A clash "between those who want freedom, justice, and equality and those who want to continue the systems of exploitation."

Drawing lessons from a century and a half of struggle, this book helps us understand why it is the revolutionary conquest of power by the working class that will make possible the final battle for Black freedom—and open the way to a world based not on exploitation, violence, and racism, but human solidarity. A socialist world. $20. Also in Spanish and French.

EXPAND *your Revolutionary Library*

The Working Class and the Transformation of Learning
The Fraud of Education Reform under Capitalism
JACK BARNES

"Until society is reorganized so that education is a human activity from the time we are very young until the time we die, there will be no education worthy of working, creating humanity." $3. Also in Spanish, French, Swedish, Icelandic, Farsi, and Greek.

Capitalism's World Disorder
Working-Class Politics at the Millennium
JACK BARNES

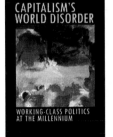

Social devastation and financial panic, coarsening of politics, cop brutality, imperialist aggression—all are products not of something gone wrong with capitalism but of its lawful workings. Yet the future can be changed by the united struggle of workers and farmers conscious of their capacity to wage revolutionary battles for state power and transform the world. $25. Also in Spanish and French.

Capitalism and the Transformation of Africa
Reports from Equatorial Guinea
MARY-ALICE WATERS, MARTÍN KOPPEL

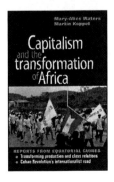

The transformation of production and class relations in a Central African country, as it is drawn deeper into the world market and both a capitalist class and modern proletariat are born. As Cuban volunteer medical brigades collaborate to transform social conditions there, the example of Cuba's socialist revolution comes alive. Woven together, the outlines of a future to be fought for today can be seen—a future in which Africa's toilers have more weight in world politics than ever before. $10. Also in Spanish.

The Cuban Revolution and

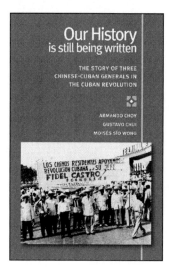

Our History Is Still Being Written
THE STORY OF THREE CHINESE-CUBAN GENERALS
IN THE CUBAN REVOLUTION

In Cuba, the greatest measure against racial
discrimination "was the revolution itself,"
says Gen. Moisés Sío Wong, "the triumph of a
socialist revolution." Armando Choy, Gustavo
Chui, and Sío Wong talk about the historic place
of Chinese immigration to Cuba, as well as
more than five decades of revolutionary action
and internationalism, from Cuba to Angola
and Venezuela today. Through their stories we
see how millions of ordinary men and women
changed the course of history, becoming
different human beings in the process. $20. Also
in Spanish and Chinese.

From the Escambray to the Congo
IN THE WHIRLWIND OF THE CUBAN REVOLUTION
Víctor Dreke

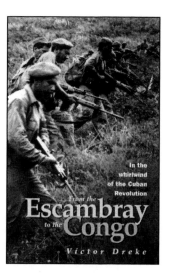

The author describes how easy it became after
the Cuban Revolution to take down a rope
segregating blacks from whites in the town
square, yet how enormous was the battle to
transform social relations underlying all the
"ropes" inherited from capitalism and Yankee
domination. Dreke, second in command of the
internationalist column in the Congo led by
Che Guevara in 1965, recounts the creative joy
with which working people have defended their
revolutionary course—from Cuba's Escambray
mountains to Africa and beyond. $17. Also in
Spanish.

Renewal or Death
Fidel Castro

"To really establish total equality takes more than declaring it in law," Fidel Castro
told delegates to the 1986 congress of the Cuban Communist Party, pointing to the
revolution's enormous conquests in the fight against anti-black racism. "We can't
leave it to chance to correct historical injustices," he said. "We have to straighten
out what history has twisted." In *New International* no. 6. $16

World Politics

The First and Second
Declarations of Havana

Manifestos of
revolutionary struggle
in the Americas
adopted by the Cuban people

The First and Second Declarations of Havana

Nowhere are the questions of revolutionary strategy that today confront men and women on the front lines of struggles in the Americas addressed with greater truthfulness and clarity than in these two documents, adopted by million-strong assemblies of the Cuban people in 1960 and 1962. These uncompromising indictments of imperialist plunder and "the exploitation of man by man" continue to stand as manifestos of revolutionary struggle by working people the world over. $10. Also in Spanish, French, and Arabic.

Che Guevara Talks to Young People

The Argentine-born revolutionary leader challenges youth of Cuba and the world to study, to work, to become disciplined. To join the front lines of struggles, small and large. To politicize themselves and the work of their organizations. To become a different kind of human being as they strive with working people of all lands to transform the world. Eight talks from 1959 to 1964. $15. Also in Spanish.

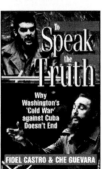

To Speak the Truth

WHY WASHINGTON'S 'COLD WAR' AGAINST CUBA DOESN'T END

Fidel Castro, Ernesto Che Guevara

In historic speeches before the United Nations General Assembly and other UN bodies, Guevara and Castro address the peoples of the world, explaining why the U.S. government fears the example of the socialist revolution in Cuba and why Washington's effort to destroy it will fail. $17

www.pathfinderpress.com

New International

A MAGAZINE OF MARXIST POLITICS AND THEORY

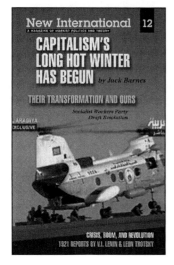

NEW INTERNATIONAL NO. 12

CAPITALISM'S LONG HOT WINTER HAS BEGUN

Jack Barnes

and "Their Transformation and Ours," Resolution of the Socialist Workers Party

Today's sharpening interimperialist conflicts are fueled both by the opening stages of what will be decades of economic, financial, and social convulsions and class battles, and by the most far-reaching shift in Washington's military policy and organization since the U.S. buildup toward World War II. Class-struggle-minded working people must face this historic turning point for imperialism, and draw satisfaction from being "in their face" as we chart a revolutionary course to confront it. $16

NEW INTERNATIONAL NO. 14

REVOLUTION, INTERNATIONALISM, AND SOCIALISM: THE LAST YEAR OF MALCOLM X

Jack Barnes

"To understand Malcolm's last year is to see how, in the imperialist epoch, revolutionary leadership of the highest political capacity, courage, and integrity converges with communism. That truth has even greater weight today as billions around the world, in city and countryside, from China to Brazil, are being hurled into the modern class struggle by the violent expansion of world capitalism."—Jack Barnes

Also in No. 14: "The Clintons' Antilabor Legacy: Roots of the 2008 World Financial Crisis"; "The Stewardship of Nature Also Falls to the Working Class"; and "Setting the Record Straight on Fascism and World War II." $14

ALL THESE ISSUES ARE ALSO AVAILABLE IN SPANISH AND MOST IN FRENCH AT
WWW.PATHFINDERPRESS.COM

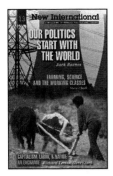

NEW INTERNATIONAL NO. 13

OUR POLITICS
START WITH THE WORLD

Jack Barnes

The huge economic and cultural inequalities between imperialist and semicolonial countries, and among classes within almost every country, are produced, reproduced, and accentuated by the workings of capitalism. For vanguard workers to build parties able to lead a successful revolutionary struggle for power in our own countries, says Jack Barnes in the lead article, our activity must be guided by a strategy to close this gap.

Also: "Farming, Science, and the Working Classes" *by Steve Clark.* $14

NEW INTERNATIONAL NO. 11

U.S. IMPERIALISM HAS LOST THE COLD WAR

Jack Barnes

Contrary to imperialist expectations at the opening of the 1990s in the wake of the collapse of regimes across Eastern Europe and the USSR claiming to be communist, the workers and farmers there have not been crushed. The toilers remain an intractable obstacle to imperialism's advance, one the exploiters will have to confront in class battles and war. $16

NEW INTERNATIONAL NO. 8

CHE GUEVARA, CUBA, AND THE ROAD TO SOCIALISM

Articles by Ernesto Che Guevara, Carlos Rafael Rodríguez, Carlos Tablada, Mary-Alice Waters, Steve Clark, Jack Barnes

Exchanges from the opening years of the Cuban Revolution and today on the political perspectives defended by Guevara as he helped lead working people to advance the transformation of economic and social relations in Cuba. $10

NEW INTERNATIONAL NO. 5

THE COMING REVOLUTION
IN SOUTH AFRICA

Jack Barnes

Writing a decade before the white supremacist regime fell, Barnes explores the social roots of apartheid in South African capitalism and tasks of urban and rural toilers in dismantling it, as they forge a communist leadership of the working class. $14

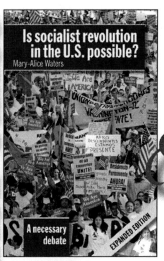

Is Socialist Revolution in the U.S. Possible?
A Necessary Debate
MARY-ALICE WATERS

In two talks, presented as part of a wide-ranging debate at the Venezuela International Book Fairs in 2007 and 2008, Waters explains why a socialist revolution in the United States is possible. Why revolutionary struggles by working people are inevitable, forced upon us by the crisis-driven assaults of the propertied classes. As solidarity grows among a fighting vanguard of working people, the outlines of coming class battles can already be seen. $7. Also in Spanish and French.

Cuba and the Coming American Revolution
JACK BARNES

The Cuban Revolution of 1959 had a worldwide political impact, including on working people and youth in the imperialist heartland. As the mass, proletarian-based struggle for Black rights was already advancing in the U.S., the social transformation fought for and won by the Cuban toilers set an example that socialist revolution is not only necessary—it can be made and defended. This second edition, with a new foreword by Mary-Alice Waters, should be read alongside *Is Socialist Revolution in the U.S. Possible?* $10. Also in Spanish and French.

Revolutionary Continuity
Marxist Leadership in the U.S.
FARRELL DOBBS

How successive generations of fighters joined in the struggles that shaped the U.S. labor movement, seeking to build a class-conscious revolutionary leadership capable of advancing the interests of workers and small farmers and linking up with fellow toilers worldwide. 2 vols. *The Early Years: 1848–1917,* $20; *Birth of the Communist Movement: 1918–1922,* $19.

www.pathfinderpress.com